DIANA

A PRINCESS FOR THE WORLD

DIANA

A PRINCESS FOR THE WORLD

By
Martine Kurz
and
Christine Gauthey

BARNES & NOBLE
BOOKS
NEW YORK

This edition published by Barnes & Noble, Inc., by arrangement with
Éditions de La Martinière, Paris

English-language edition created by Harry N. Abrams, Incorporated,
New York

Translated from the French by Ben Lifson

Typography: Tina Thompson

Photographs by Gamma

Printed and bound in France

1997 Barnes & Noble Books

ISBN 0–7607–0886–X

Sixty million flowers. In front of Kensington Palace, where Diana lived during the last months of her life, the harsh macadam is transformed into an immense rose garden. With thorns—symbolic of the life of this tender-hearted princess mourned today by sixty million Britons. At thirty-six, beautiful, radiant, and, finally, love-fulfilled. How could the world have anticipated that sad August night that turned someone so human into a legend?

Born into the high British aristocracy, reared in sumptuous family residences and playing as a girl in the gardens of the royal castle of Sandringham, Diana could have followed paths laid out by generations of women of her station: carefree childhood, rich marriage, frivolous existence—at a thousand-mile remove from human suffering. But in 1980, the moment her idyll with the heir to the throne became known, it was a shy, fragile girl who pressed herself awkwardly against Charles, with whom she was, without a doubt, profoundly in love. The hearts of Britain—of the whole world!—melted. Why? Because we are mad about any lovely fairy tale. But above all because for the first time, a member of the royal family displayed human qualities and weaknesses, uninhibited by her status—as if she were anyone else.

Diana was all that the Windsors are not: impish, blushing, shy, spontaneous, and full of a zest for life. Natural. What did it matter that she was still only a girl? Within the chrysalis stirs the butterfly. Finally, her vocation as a kindergarten teacher, lovingly practiced, tumbled the last barriers separating her from the people. Did Diana crave love madly? The British asked nothing more than to offer it.

It was love at first sight, they for her and she for them. And for her, so desperate for affection, every public appearance from that moment on was daunting since she was so shy, yet encouraging because of her universally warm reception. All those hands stretched out to her, how could she not press them, take sustenance from their warmth? In the jubilation that followed her marriage to Charles, Diana was so appealing to the people that, unbeknown to her, she herself offered the royal gift to the family to which she would thenceforth belong. Thanks to her, the Windsors regained the humanity, warmth, and spontaneity that had faded from their lives since World War II. Didn't Charles go so far as to give, in public, and for the first time in the history of the monarchy, a furtive kiss to the future queen of England? Thanks to Diana, the people had the impression that everything was going to change.

Thenceforth and with great emotion, Britons followed her apprenticeship as Her Royal Highness. Diana showed herself to be touching, a woman of good will, grace, and kindness. And when she gave birth to William, heir apparent to the crown, she became indeed the princess of hearts. When a second son, Harry, was born in 1984, Diana fulfilled all the expectations of Her Majesty's subjects, all the more so since she showed herself to be an exemplary mother, challenging protocol many times for the sake of her children's happiness. For them the princess was simply a mom who smiled, ran, grumbled, reassured, bathed them, pampered them, and, just like any mother, unaffectedly participated in their first days at school after holidays, with sneakers on her feet, scant makeup, satchel in her hand. Thus the British had the impression of glimpsing her privacy and seeing her on an equal footing. And if from time to time the magazines' glossy pages changed Diana back into their crown princess and she thus slipped away from them a little, they only loved her the more for it. Her beauty, supreme elegance, and the admiration that she inspired were so many honors that they received through her. Surely it was she who re-gilded the nation's blazon. Sometimes, of course, she seemed out of touch; her giddiness, her increasingly frequent rebellions against the photographers who stalked her, the millions spent on frills, all this frivolity squared poorly with the day-to-day reality of a country mired in unemployment and economic crisis. Later, rumors of her having lovers began to circulate, and they proved true. Diana was unfaithful, and for the first time the English felt betrayed, let down by one who, until then, had brought them only pride and joy. Her marriage to Charles might as well be over, and not just implicitly so—after all, he too had publicly acknowledged his affair with Camilla Parker-Bowles: eyebrows were being raised. But here again, Diana's spontaneity and profound confusion would rally the people to her cause. For it was a humiliated and wounded woman who could admit, "Yes, I have sinned." Tears ran down her cheeks. And the nonplussed British railed against the cold Charles. If their princess suffered so, it must be all his fault, many believed. Thus Diana regained the path to their hearts—all their hearts: children, the sick, the aged, the downtrodden, the handicapped.... What she had begun to learn earlier through her charity work was reaffirmed now: her mission on earth was the giving of love.

A little more every day. With a simple caress from her fingertips, a murmured word, or an attentive glance. Diana had soothing power. What difference does it make if it's only for an instant, a drop of water in the ocean of Third World misery, a whisper drowned out by the din of bombs, by famine? Giving is the important thing. In the final months in the Princess's appointment book, trips piled up: she wanted to do good everywhere. For it was only this that made her happy.

This and the promise of a new love. At last the British could hope for her happiness: their princess would be cherished as she deserved by a prince charming whom no protocol could either stifle or check. At long last the fairy tale was to be recaptured, a great story that would last long, long.... The two lovers loved before the eyes of the world, on luxury yachts, under burning summer suns—their last suns, their final summer.

Stars are not extinguished in winter, after a sad, gloomy December night. Diana departed on the last day of August, on a warm, mild night, in the world's most beautiful city, thus proving that princesses are fragile and ephemeral beings. Flowers that live and die in a morning's span.

From Aristocratic Childhood To Royal Marriage

Lady Diana Frances Spencer was born on July 1, 1961, to a family at the heart of the British aristocracy. Even as a child she showed herself sweet yet head-strong, conscious of the obligatory respect for codes of behavior proper to her rank, yet all the while seeking to preserve a dearly bought autonomy. She was a real angel—when not opposed, said one of her playmates. And this is the entire tension of Diana's childhood: that of a young person of the best society who tries to keep her head above water and remain true to herself while weathering family storms.

Diana was the third daughter of Viscount Althorp Spencer, later the eighth Earl Spencer, who until 1954 served as equerry to the Queen, a position granted only to the upper nobility. Among her ancestors Diana counted two kings, numerous dukes and counts, and she was Prince Charles's cousin eleven times removed.

Diana passed her early years in the company of her older sisters, Sarah and Jane, and her younger brother, Charles, going back and forth between the paternal estate of Althorp House and the sumptuous residence of Park House, in Norfolk, a hop, skip, and a jump from the Royal Castle of Sandringham. She was very close to her mother, Frances Roche—whom she closely resembled, according to the nurse who reared mother and daughter both—and she suffered from her parents' failed relationship (Viscount Althorp was twelve years Frances's senior). Arguments multiplied and became harsher. Even little Charles's birth in 1964 didn't succeed in averting the separation.

When her parents divorced in 1969, the already troubled world of childhood collapsed for Diana. She was deeply hurt by her mother's departure and remarriage to Peter Shand Kydd, rich heir to a great wallpaper concern. The divorce battle was particularly rough in respect to the custody of the children, which in the end went to Lord Spencer. The children then felt abandoned by their mother, who followed her lover to London and then Scotland. They saw her on weekends and during vacations.

Diana changed. She took upon herself the responsibility for her little brother's well-being and tried to protect him from the suffering she had endured. Her close friends see in this period the origins of her affinity for young children and vulnerable people generally. But it was also during this time that she herself became increasingly vulnerable.

From this experience she was to retain a deep feeling of insecurity, which led her to try all possible means for filling the void left by Lady Frances.

Her second major childhood shock was her father's remarriage, in 1977, to Raine, former Countess of Dartmouth and daughter of the famous novelist Barbara Cartland. Even though Diana nourished herself with the romantic dreams of Barbara Cartland's books, she bore up badly under this intrusive effort to replace her mother.

The smiling child was transformed into a sullen adolescent. At fifteen, after attending boarding schools, where she was appreciated more for her good citizenship than for her scholastic achievement, she was sent to Switzerland. There she went to finishing school and perfected her French before returning to London for more practical studies. She studied cooking and landed her first job as a cook in the school where, a few weeks later, she became a kindergarten teacher.

Thenceforth Diana led the life of a modern young woman. She shared an apartment with two friends in Earl's Court, a neighborhood in West London, drove her red Mini Metro around London, wore jeans, and listened to pop music (formerly forbidden by her stepmother). Diana became a young woman of her generation and was admired for her vocational dedication. She regained some of the spontaneity and noisy gaiety of childhood. Gossip attributed no flings to her, no secret love affairs either.

Having belonged from childhood to that set of the high aristocracy's children traditionally chosen as playmates for heirs to the throne, she had known Charles since she was a young girl. At sixteen she became reacquainted with him; Charles was then a guest of her eldest sister, Sarah, whom he dated for several months.

The young Diana was intimidated; she blushed when the Prince's eyes fell on her. But according to Emma Roblès, one of Diana's biographers, Diana dreamed that one day she would become Princess of Wales. With her gentleness and charm, she would win the Prince's affections.

If it is difficult to know with certainty what motivated Diana at the time of this crucial meeting, her goal was more obvious during the summer of 1980, when she encountered Charles again after having seen him only very infrequently in the last three years. It was in Scotland, at Balmoral, where the royal family traditionally goes to spend the summer, that our modern Cinderella once more met up with the prince charming of her adolescent dreams. Diana came to pay a visit to her sister Jane, who is married to the Queen's private secretary and had just had a baby. Charles himself was later to confess surprise at discovering, in Diana, a young woman at once so natural, simple, and urbane. She was charming because of her own special alchemy of attributes, a mixture of spontaneity, candor, and delicate courtesy. She loved to laugh but knew how to keep silent; she knew how to be independent but respected the traditions of her class; and although possessed of a wild romanticism, she had not yet given her heart away. According to Andrew Morton, another biographer of Diana's, "Charles saw Diana with new eyes. Suddenly, as she later told her friends, she found herself overwhelmed by his enthusiastic affections.... From that point, their relationship began to develop."

On the dawn of her twentieth year, Lady Di—or, as the British people who had already adopted her now called her, "Shy Di"—saw all the doors to her dreams opening before her.

Balmoral is made for idylls. The royal grounds offer vacationers all the charm of Scotland, its hills of heather and its pine forests. It was in this dreamscape that Diana saw her wishes granted.

She came into the heir apparent's life just at the time that he was under increasing pressure to find a bride. He wanted to escape the mournful solitude into which he had plunged after his break with his first love, Camilla. This young woman, whom the royal family never considered capable of meeting the specifications of a wife to majesty, had turned her back on her lover in order to be united in lawful wedlock to the cavalry lieutenant Andrew Parker-Bowles.

In Diana, Charles found a freshness that moved and charmed him. The love that this early childhood teacher avowed for the children she cared for melted the heart of the most intractable of the Windsors.

Diana moved people by her tenacity, her wild will to realize her dream. Above all she wanted a wholly successful marriage and to start a family—preferably a royal one—and to break with the sad image of a childhood torn between an absent mother and a much-too-present stepmother.

She knew that Charles was thirteen years her senior, and that this difference almost exactly corresponded to the one that existed between her parents. But so what? Youth overwhelmed reason.

Charles reasoned similarly; that is, he didn't reason at all. He let himself be led by and to the dream-path that Diana proffered him, and thought in this way to definitively turn over a new leaf and at the same time to fulfill his obligation as crown prince: to join in a marriage that would produce an heir, first to the country of Wales and, later, to the United Kingdom.

For months the most observed couple in England maintained an obligatory reserve—played the game. To journalists the Prince of Wales would answer, "You will know in good time," whereas Lady Diana would declare—perfectly observing protocol—"I can neither invalidate nor validate." However, the press was very much aware that this particular love affair could turn out to be much more serious than its predecessors.

On February 24, Buckingham Palace officially announced that Charles and Diana were engaged. Once again Diana's life changed. Serene and somber before the armies of photographers who would await her in front of her house, she was as spontaneous and sentimental as always with her friends. When the TV news came on she would call to her roommates, "Come quick, they're talking about us on the telly!" For the future princess the dream was still intact.

But in order to join the Windsor clan she had to meet the requirements appropriate to her rank.

With the help of the palace guards, the young woman moved and settled into Clarence House, the Queen Mother's residence, until her Kensington Palace apartment would be ready. She exchanged her little red car for an official Rolls. And she received on occasion the counsel of the Queen, who had undertaken to put the finishing touches on her education and to teach her court usages and customs before the wedding.

If Diana consented with good grace (more or less) to learn the history of the House of Windsor or the most royal way to greet a chief of state, she never resolved to respect the severely restrictive atmosphere of the royal palace.

But Lady Di had become so popular in such a short time that even the Queen Mother winked at certain acts of bravado, deciding to consider them temporary.

Diana was radiant. As her sole jewel she wore the engagement ring Charles had given her: a sumptuous sapphire enhanced by diamonds. It had "horrified" a Labor deputy because the announcement of the engagement coincided with one concerning a rise in unemployment, but it ravished the public, who in fact needed something to dream about in order to forget the unemployment. England's eternal contradictions...

The wedding was set for July 29, 1981, and it was Camilla Parker-Bowles who was chosen to accompany Diana on her shopping trips. Albeit caught in a trap comprised, on the one side, of her future husband's former mistress (whose relationship with Charles plagued Diana with fear and jealousy throughout the engagement) and, on the other, a Queen somewhat annoyed by her much-too-beautiful daughter-in-law's sudden popularity, Diana didn't let it show. She did everything in her power to give her wedding the panache and brilliance of a dream. For this, as well as for her soaring beauty, her incredible willingness to believe in great love, and her natural need to share her happiness, England loved her.

At last the young woman realized her dream, accepting with equal generosity both the joys and the constraints of the princess trade. Doubtless she had not reckoned with either the magnitude of the task before her or the solitude that already lay in wait for her.

And so on July 29, 1981, Lady Diana became the world's most photographed woman: more than 750 million television viewers watched the wedding ceremony of the young woman and the prince.

The betrothal: the roundness of Diana's ring—a sapphire set with diamonds—
tempers Charles's austere coat of arms like a promise of mutual happiness.

Opposite:
The first official photograph of the engaged couple in Buckingham Palace garden:
Diana's smile already ravishes the photographers.

On this 29th of July, 1981, a pumpkin-turned-coach carries one who is still
only the daughter of an equerry to Queen Elizabeth
toward her royal destiny…

Opposite:
The whole world views Diana's sumptuous wedding dress, a creation of
the young British designers David and Elisabeth Emmanuel.

The bells of St. Paul's cathedral peal in quick succession and the audience holds its breath
while Diana, tenderly escorted by her father, Lord Spencer, approaches the altar.

Opposite:
The serious face of Charles as he says "I do."

Above:
In a few moments, on the balcony of Buckingham Palace, Charles will give his young bride
a kiss that will mark a unique moment in the history of the monarchy: the first kiss
given in public by a Prince of Wales to a future Queen of England.

To the acclamations of a jubilant crowd, the young married couple rides through London in the royal landau.

Unlike most young newlyweds in the world,
they will not enjoy their honeymoon on some distant isle…
Their trip, punctuated by official appearances, is all royal duty.

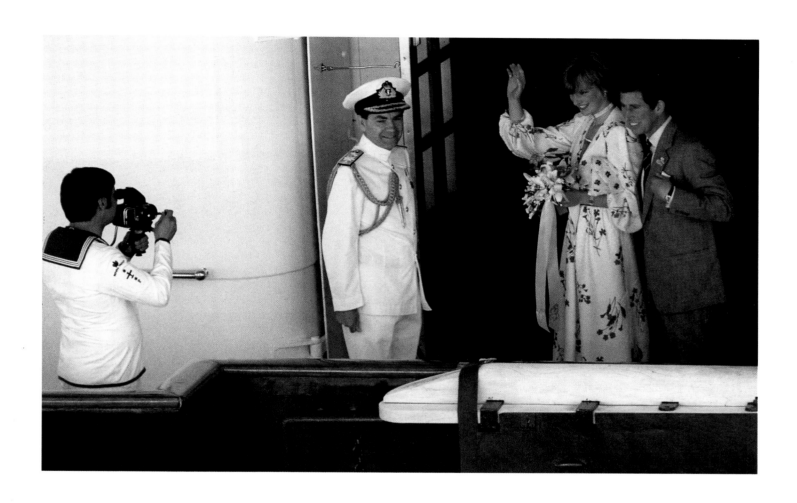

The kingdom gives
an ovation to Diana,
who is pregnant
with William I, heir
to the crown!

Diana poses in October 1984 for official photographs holding baby Harry.

Under the proud eyes of daddy Charles, Harry's great-grandmother, the Queen Mother,
and his grandmother, Queen Elizabeth, Diana adjusts the frills of the little prince's dress. December 1984.

The royal couple leaving the hospital where Diana has just given birth
to a second son, Harry, September 15, 1984.

Opposite:
Baby Harry with his loving father, great-grandmother, and grandmother.

Diana in her favorite role. Nothing makes her happier than spending time with her sons.

For their sake she will defy protocol, rejecting both overstrict governesses and excessively austere boarding schools.

Behind rain-drenched
windows, Diana gives
her famous smile to the
British who have come
to cheer her. Her child's
little hand tries its first
official salute.

The Princess of Wales always appreciated the Queen Mother's joyous, playful sense of humor.
Here they are shown at Buckingham Palace, June 1991.

Opposite:
With William and Harry, August 1988, Highgrove.

Hitting the road early on bicycles, June 1989.

Opposite:
Holiday time for a family almost just like every other. In August of 1988,
a stay in Palma at the house of the Spanish royal family.

Diana wouldn't have missed this festivity for the whole world: the mother's race organized by William's primary school. Moreover, she's the first to cross the finish line—royal and barefoot. June 1989.

As is the custom at the beginning of school, Diana has faithfully accompanied William to his first day of class ever since he was accepted at the famous prep school of Eton. Here even Charles and Harry lend their support. September 1995.

Opposite: Diana and her sons, August 1995.

The royal family on the occasion of William's confirmation ceremony, March 5, 1997.

The royal couple, April 1993.

The Couple With Two Faces

When she married Charles, Diana didn't know that English kings don't give up their infidelities. Especially not in the House of Windsor. Edward VII, for instance, son of the famous Queen Victoria, reveled in Belle Epoque naughtiness and tarts.

Charles also had points in common with Edward VIII, who gave up the throne in order to marry the twice-divorced American Wallis Simpson. But Charles seems more like a hypocrite. He married Diana but didn't renounce his mistress, Camilla Parker-Bowles, whose shadow fell on the young Princess of Wales. Diana did not at first suspect its menace. Not for a moment, not even during the engagement, did Charles envisage a break with the mistress who had intoxicated him for years. Camilla went as far as advising him to choose Diana, thinking that "the little dumbbell" would take it lying down rather than end up one day a king's jealous wife. Everyone was fooled.

In the first months of her marriage Diana discovered that it wasn't good form to laugh and joke during the traditional public appearances in which she and her husband had to participate. First false note: the Highland Games. Her husband wears a kilt, and she herself dresses Scottish. Diana giggles, Charles looks complicitous, then shifts to his austere attitude, second nature to him now, and Diana lowers her eyes—an attitude that will shortly become second nature to her. The young Princess, though now pregnant (William was born eleven months after the wedding), continued the weight-loss that had begun when she was engaged. However, domestics at Buckingham Palace, where the young couple lived at the beginning of their union, sometimes came upon Diana in the kitchens, stuffing herself with cake. "Poor thing," they thought, "she must not dare eat according to her appetite at official dinners." Which was in part true. But it was more serious than that. These, in fact, were the first signs of bulimia, a common-enough illness among adolescents who feel inadequately loved. Bulimia is an illness that expresses itself in an abnormal devouring of anything one can put in one's mouth and is within arm's reach, but without taking pleasure in it, and hardly tasting it. Bloated with everything and above all by her guilty conscience, Diana, like all bulimics, would force herself to vomit. Quite obviously, in a palace where every action is spied upon, her pathological behavior was common knowledge in no time.

Diana hated Buckingham Palace with its four hundred twenty-nine rooms, where three hundred thirty-five largely unseen employees go about their business, almost all of them, valets and chamber maids excepted, the sons and daughters of the aristocracy. Although she herself had been brought up in the best traditions, the young princess wondered if it wasn't unreasonable for Prince Charles to be obliged to send a written note to the Queen's secretary asking to see his own mother. She vowed that her children, the first of which was soon to be born, would not be reared in the same way. And curiously enough, reports now have it that Diana's sons often played hide and seek in the Buckingham Palace corridors and that Queen Elizabeth was delighted. But toward the Princess of Wales herself the disposition of her royal mother-in-law was quite another thing. Once, for instance, Diana went down to the kitchen to give orders directly to the staff: a deplorable notion that the Queen, at once and firmly, told her to put out of her mind.

The apprenticeship of a princess is difficult. Diana had to stop moving her head and her hands when she talked. Any large gesture was forbidden a Royal Highness. Oliver Everett, second private secretary to Charles, taught Diana how to walk according to the requirements of her rank. Buckingham Palace ballroom was their practice field. As for Diana, she preferred dancing, running, swimming, diving. Luckily, the Palace has a swimming pool, so it was often with dripping hair that she was seen going up to the royal apartments, happy for her few minutes of freedom.

Diana hadn't yet guessed that the age difference between her and the Prince—thirteen years—would place such a determining weight on their union. Yet even during their honeymoon on the royal yacht, the *Britannia,* she was unnerved by Charles's inattentiveness and unromantic behavior toward her; he dozed all morning on a deck chair while she burned off energy by jogging around the deck, listening to her Walkman. But Charles's "languor" had another cause. He was far from Camilla, whose photo never left his wallet. One can imagine Diana, made anxious by a certain coolness (due to the Prince's education? or a lack of passion?), going through her husband's pockets. Unthinkable, but entirely feminine. Or she could equally well have come in suddenly on telephone conversations that promptly ended upon her entering their apartment.

After their wedding trip, the couple joined the Queen and the rest of the royal family at Balmoral. According to Morton, it was then that "the full impact of life as Princess of Wales began to hit home.... For the watching world, she smiled and laughed, seeming perfectly delighted with her new husband and new-found status.... However...the couple argued continually, [and] she lived on an emotional see-saw."

Back in London, Charles and Diana moved to Kensington Palace, but this change of surroundings solved nothing. Charles had his friends, but they weren't to Diana's taste; furthermore, hunting and polo bored her. However, tit for tat: Charles was deeply displeased by Diana's friends, whom he found pretentious and overly preoccupied by business and money.

The birth of William, on June 21, 1982, preserved appearances and the royal family seemed reconciled around the cradle—for a while. Diana became temperamental and wanted to make changes everywhere. Unable to affect the Windsors' behavior, she made the Kensington staff jump. It's said that in ten years' time over forty people left Charles and Diana's employ, implying Diana was a demanding mistress. Evenings, Charles enjoyed listening to classical music. Diana missed her rock and roll, her night clubs. Her sole companion was her friend Carolyn, with whom she had shared an apartment before her engagement, and whom she sometimes visited in the evening. After their nighttime escapades she would cloister herself like a boarding-school girl confined to quarters. Or she and Carolyn would stuff themselves with scrambled eggs and trade gossip about old boyfriends.

As for Charles, when his telephone conversations were taped and disclosed in the press many years later, it became known that he was still seeing Camilla. Their remarks are edifying.

The birth of Prince Harry, on September 15, 1984, delighted not only the Princess but, yet one more time, the whole family—which in July 1986 would include another newcomer, Sarah Ferguson, Prince Andrew's bride. The difficulties they encountered in the face of royal protocol drew Diana and Sarah together. Their wild laughter calmed anxious observers. But very soon the two sisters-in-law's intimacy annoyed the Queen, and it was Fergie who gave fresh fuel to the fire of her anger. They called her too fat, said her hair was too red, that she was too vulgar.

Charles fled, took refuge at Balmoral, painted, hunted, fished—when he wasn't visiting Highgrove, his country estate, where Camilla would secretly join him. Diana holed up at Kensington with her children, who alone still knew how to make her smile. Charles grew jealous, but only of his wife's popularity, which put him in the shade. For whatever she did, the world cheered her.

Years pass. They meet, but only for official ceremonies or trips. Anyone could see that they never spoke a word to each other. In July 1991 they seemed to celebrate their tenth wedding anniversary with some affection, but a bomb exploded a few months later.

In June 1992 the biographer Andrew Morton, known to the English court, published the book *Diana: Her True Story*. The United Kingdom was indignant—as was, indeed, the whole world, for the book was released internationally. It seemed scarcely credible at first. In it the author sets down, item by item, the Princess of Wales's heartbreaks, as told by those close to Diana. She made five suicide attempts, says Morton, one by throwing herself from the heights of a Sandringham staircase while she was pregnant with William. Charles, who was getting ready to go horseback riding, didn't change his plans. Another time she threw herself against a window at Kensington Palace. She also slit the veins of her wrists, tearing at them with blows from a pair of scissors.... Outbursts that Charles dismissed as manipulative attention-seeking and Diana explained as cries for help.

But her husband remained absolutely unmoved by these tragic domestic scenes, of which two, at least, could have been fatal to the Princess. In 1986 they made an official visit to California. During that trip she warned him that she "wanted to disappear." "If you want to disappear," Charles shouted at her, "do it in private."

The book also reveals that Diana had discovered Charles's affair with Camilla before her marriage, but that it was too late to withdraw. The loving Lady Diana Spencer still thought it possible to change the world and win her husband's love. Instead, Charles would send his mistress flowers, with little notes in code: "From Fred to Gladys"—their nicknames for each other. During their honeymoon Charles wore cufflinks bearing two intertwined "C"s. And always, those telephone conversations. "No matter what happens, I'll love you forever," murmurs Charles to Camilla.

The reaction came a few years later, when Diana began to seek consolation elsewhere. A newspaper published excerpts of an amorous conversation between the Princess and a man who declares, "At midnight, upon New Year, I'll hold you so close to me...." The tape recording mentions Fergie and the voice of Diana is recognizable, lamenting her atrocious marriage.

And indeed, the "marriage of the century" proved disastrous. Prime Minister John Major announced the official separation on December 9, 1992. In fact, it had begun months earlier. Diana waited until the end of her official engagements, at the end of 1993, to announce that she was withdrawing from her duties. She called herself harrassed by the media—already! "I am affected in my public duties equally as in my personal life, and in a manner difficult to endure. At the end of this year, when I have fulfilled my calendar appointments, I will reduce the scope of the public life that I have led up until now."

The couple "shared" their children. Diana saw them on certain weekends and during a part of their vacations. She remained unhappy. At first there was no question of divorce. However, during a television interview, Charles, Prince of Wales, admitted that he had cheated on his wife. Everyone figured he meant with Camilla Parker-Bowles. Undoubtedly he felt empowered to make his adultery public because he knew that James Hewitt, an officer in the Queen's personal guard and Diana's former riding master, was about to publish *Princess in Love,* an account of his affair with the Princess of Wales.

Stunned by Hewitt's revelations, Diana too confessed on television, in November 1995, that she had "adored" Hewitt, had been "crazy in love," and that he had betrayed her.

Divorce was now inevitable. Diana and her attorneys negotiated fiercely. Once more a fight between the Queen and her daughter-in-law: what income, what title would she retain? What rank? Diana kept her title of Princess of Wales, but not that of Her Royal Highness; she also retained her Kensington residence and was awarded a large compensatory indemnity. On February 27, 1996, Charles and Diana's last tête-à-tête as spouses lasted three-quarters of an hour. The decree ending their marriage was handed down on August 28, 1996, by the London divorce courts.

Diana, who had spent Christmas of 1995 by herself, celebrated the 1996 holidays in the Caribbean with William and Harry. At last she could choose places she liked. In the sun. The summer of 1997 was charged with madness. She began to see Dodi al-Fayed, an Egyptian millionaire whose father, Mohammed al-Fayed, owns the legendary Ritz Hotel—where she had the last meal of her life—and the Harrods department store, a London institution. In broad daylight, on the deck of Dodi's yacht, Diana let her new passion blaze forth—not only for Dodi but for his family. The British establishment had humiliated them by denying them British citizenship; stiff Britain had rejected them, as it had Diana. And so not only did Diana find happiness with them but this new chapter of her life could be titled, "A Princess's Revenge," with, sadly, the words "The End" inscribed therein. But from beyond death, Diana has left such a mark on the monarchy that it will never be the same.

The post-Diana world is in progress. The eyes of Britain and the rest of the world are focused on the royal family. Diana's flame burns brightly.

Opposite:
Seville, April 1985.

Right:
A kilted, long-stockinged Charles shows his fiancée around the beloved lands of Balmoral—a wild and melancholy region that she, however, will never come to love.

Venice: a time of love, folklore, and fantasy. May 1985.

Opposite:
The royal couple in Scotland for Charles's birthday, November 14, 1985.

Charles and Diana in
Italy, April 1985.

Diana and Charles
in Germany, November
1987.

The whirlwind of official appearances: attentive, winning, or mischievous —the famous look from the corner of Diana's eye shows up every time. Here, the couple in Canada, May 1986.

Charles and Diana in
Qatar, November 1986.

A cup and a kiss for the Princess from her polo champion. Even though she didn't particularly like the sport, she was at Charles's side at every important match.

Opposite:

They already had little left to say to each other, but Diana ran to Charles's bedside
when he was hurt during a polo match in August 1990.

Above:

The couple in Hungary, May 1990.

Charles and Diana in May 1993, at the memorial of the battle of the Atlantic.

Visiting a military cemetery, Prague, May 1991.

In the deafening roar of cannons, Diana explodes with laughter. December 1993.

Even in public—as here, during a trip to Canada in 1995—Diana and Charles no longer feign love for one another.

White House guests of the Reagans, November 1985:
the Princess will charm the Americans by dancing to rock music with…John Travolta.

President François Mitterrand gazes at the beaming Diana. Paris, November 1988.

The Vatican: Pope John-Paul II
grants Charles and Diana an
audience in 1985.

With Paul McCartney, her girlhood idol. Lille, November 1992.

Opposite:
The Princess meets Tom Cruise and his wife, Nicole Kidman, at the opening of *Far and Away*, August 1992.
Diana had great admiration for Cruise—she and William later went to a shooting of *Mission Impossible* at Pinewood Studios.

Diana going to a reception at
the London Palladium,
December 1990.

Opposite:
London, January 1992.

At fifteen she won the dance contest at her school. Years later,
dancing was still one of her favorite pastimes. January 1988.

Opposite:
Great Britain, February 1987.

Diana on a tour of
Wales, May 1991.

At the opening of *Shirley Valentine*, October 1989.

The Princess at a charity gala in London, June 1990, and
in November 1991 at the opening of *Hot Shots*.

Diana, Liberty

1982. When she left London's St. Mary's Hospital with her son William, in her carmine dress and with her hair falling to her shoulders, Diana looked more like an American soap-opera heroine than a modern princess.

For three years she tried to adapt her style to that of the English court. With a succession of wide-brimmed hats—and hats of all styles—she had a look just a bit too flashy to be real. She wore brightly colored dresses, relatively long.

In 1985, after the birth of her second son, Harry, the year before, Diana began to assert herself. Since her husband, the Prince of Wales, didn't so much as look at her anymore, she had only to please herself, or more exactly, her taste. She began to emphasize her long legs, which she would stretch out marvelously in front of her as she got out of a car. At last she did what felt good to her. Farewell, protocol. At the White House she danced to rock and roll with John Travolta in front of the amused Nancy and Ronald Reagan.

From year to year, precisely as her love story disintegrated, she found her style. Her face grew finer. Away with the bangs that hid her forehead. And a more sober elegance began to unite with the noble sadness that she evinced.

She regained that smile that drove the whole world mad, but only when in the company of her children or engaged in her charity work. Then she radiated happiness.

Opposite:
Wales, October 1981.

94

Westminster, 1982.

November 1983.

April 1984.

Florence, 1985.

1985.

1985.

Florence, April 1985.

November 1986, in Bahrain.

April 1987.

November 1988.

In Australia, January 1988.

At Windsor, July 1988.

May 1991.

July 1993.

In London, 1997.

At the laying of the cornerstone at Northwick Park Hospital in London, July 1997.

Diana, Compassion

From an early age, Diana felt happy only among children. After her parents' divorce she cared for her younger brother, Charles, like a mother. It was entirely by instinct that she discovered her path in life by becoming a kindergarten teacher, the one title she never sought. From childhood she loved innocence. "I have so much to give," said this young woman whose love was rejected by Charles—who went so far as to take exception to his wife's immense popularity.

The Princess knew how to attend to children. She found words to make them smile. She caressed their cheeks and never wearied of the touch of babies' skin, of natural, tender gestures, of maternal impulses.

She took the hands of the sick and held them long in her own. The patience of little ones silently waiting for someone to come and care for them astonished her. She moved delicately with the wounded, adjusting the sheets that covered them. She cajoled, cradled, and kissed. With Diana, love for others expressed itself through touch and empathetic words. She needed to feel in contact with life, even when it held on with only a breath, in order better to transmit her energy, her faith, and her wish to soothe, to bring relief.

Opposite:
April 1991.

112

A look, a smile, or…

Opposite: Diana visits Australia, April 1983.

Above left: April 1991.

Above right: Cambridgeshire, June 1993.

South of London, November 1993.

a handshake…

London, September 1992.

from their beloved Princess...

December 1993.

and hearts melt.

Australia, November 1985.

Opposite: Westminster, May 1991.

In Nigeria, March 1990, and Kyoto, Japan, in 1986. The "Di touch" is also there:
a wide-brimmed hat, with a kimono to honor her hosts.

Australia, 1983.

Diana in Pakistan in August–September 1991, the guest of Jemina and Imran Khan.
In Lahore she visits the Shaukat Khanum hospital for cancer patients.

Trip to Pakistan, 1991.

Opposite: December 1993.

Above: June 1992.

November 1992, Annual Remembrance Day.

1983.

A Committed Princess

From the beginning of her marriage Diana, who was never at her ease at official ceremonies, preferred visits to hospitals and day-care centers to bowing and scraping to the great. Among children, the sick, and the wounded, she instinctively recovered her need to reassure and nurture.

After the couple's official separation was announced, in 1992, she granted herself many trips throughout the world that had been forbidden her by her rank of Royal Highness. She went to Brazil and to Bosnia, where she spent time among Serbian and Bosnian children. It was at her request that the tenor Luciano Pavarotti gave a concert in Sarajevo, at no fee, for the benefit of the orphans.

She went twice to Angola to protest against the use of land mines, which ravage the world: one victim every twenty minutes. "I wasn't prepared for the horror of the reality," she said. However, she gave proof of a true tenderness in respect to many, many suffering children throughout the world, for example, those who had been waiting for years for prostheses and hoped so much to learn to walk again. She confessed, "The media follow me everywhere. Best to use their interest to help those who suffer."

In the mid-1980s, she was also one of the first to denounce the generally hostile attitude toward AIDS victims. "You can shake their hands, embrace them. God knows they need it."

To encourage compassion, she kissed a young man sick with AIDS, as well as a leper. Her bounty reached sick people the world over.

Opposite: Zimbabwe, July 1993.

Visiting the sick in India, February 1992.

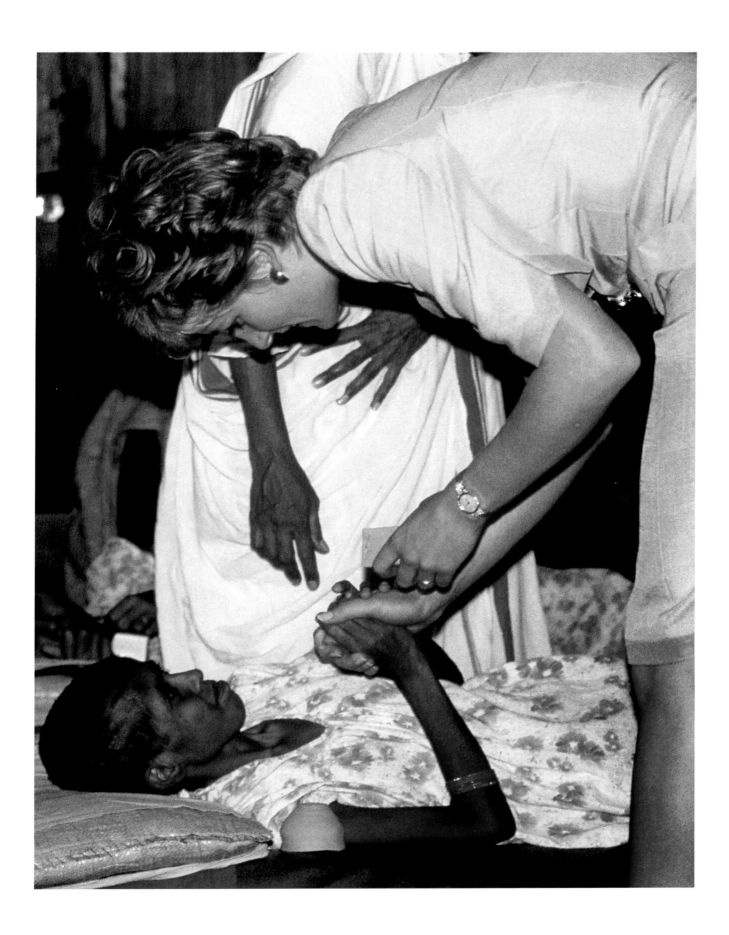

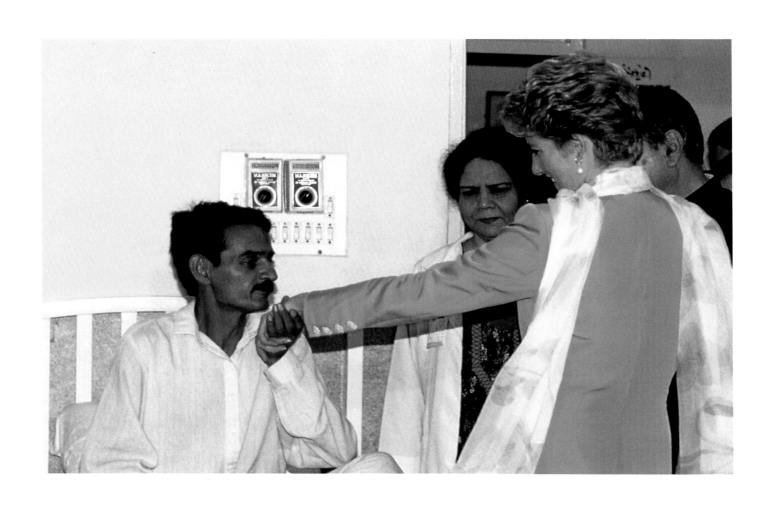

Islamabad, September 1991.
Diana couldn't stand the suffering of children or adults.

July 1991, London.

At a refugee camp in Zimbabwe, July 1993, she serves soup and plays checkers.

Smiles and comfort in Rio de Janeiro, April 1991.

Everywhere, she always had time for children.

Above: In Sarajevo, August 1997.

Opposite: In London, July 1997, at the laying of the cornerstone at Northwick Park Hospital.

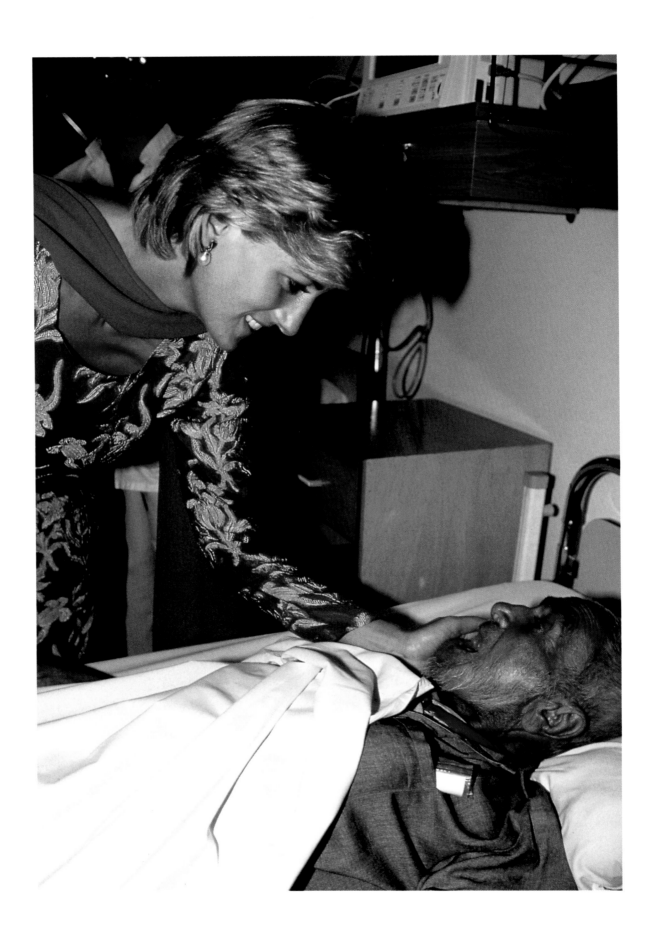

Preceding pages:
Lahore, May 1997.

Above and opposite:
The struggle to ban land mines was one of Diana's last campaigns.
Here she is accompanied by a young victim in Luanda, Angola, January 1997.

In Bosnia, she brings a bit of comfort to women whose husbands, sons, and in some cases whole families have perished during the course of the war. August 1997.

Diana in Sarajevo,
August 1997.

150

Snettingham Beach, December 1990.

Dream's End

It was a little past midnight that Sunday, August 31, 1997, when a black Mercedes sedan crashed into the thirteenth pillar of the Pont d'Alma tunnel in Paris. Diana, Princess of Wales, died two hours after being admitted to the La Pitié-Salpêtrière hospital. Two people died with her, including Dodi al-Fayed, the man she had loved in sight of the whole world for a few weeks before the crash.

With this last love, which she had delivered over to the whole press corps, the Princess had her revenge. The revenge of a woman held up to public ridicule by her husband, Prince Charles; revenge against the British monarchy, which had abandoned her to herself; revenge against the conventions that had ground her down. That night, what had begun in fairy tale ended in tragedy. A tragedy that elevated her life into the realm of legend.

Devastated by her parents' separation, she had to resign herself to divorce even though as an adolescent she had vowed never to make her children relive her own unhappiness. When she found a man to console her for her misfortunes as a spouse, she was betrayed by that lover as well, who sold their secret affair to the publisher with the highest bid. Thenceforth she became the world's most hunted person, ceaselessly pursued by paparazzi who knew that snapshots of Diana were worth far more than those of all the other stars put together. And that night it was precisely in trying to escape their lenses that she met her death, en route to the Duke and Duchess of Windsor's former private residence, which had been bought by Dodi's father. Another revenge for the Princess, who might have found herself presented with this legendary house, in which King Edward VIII resided after his abdication.

But fate didn't give her the time to savor her revenge.

Diana was thirty-six. For the sixteen years of her marriage to Charles, Prince of Wales, her life was a nightmare. And it was only a few months before that she had learned to be herself again, a rebel princess who had never entirely conformed to court protocol, who loved dancing at night clubs and preferred an Elton John concert to stuffy performances at London's Royal Albert Hall. It was as though the girl of ninteen, "chosen" by the Queen of England, had been stunted just as she began to grow up; an adolescent broken by royal selection.

Opposite:
Brisbane, Australia, April 1983.

United By Fate

They had met on several occasions and the love of humanity they shared united them. Upon the announcement of Diana's death, Mother Teresa expressed her sadness at not being able to attend the Princess's funeral because of the state of her own health. On September 5, six days after Diana's death, Mother Teresa, age eighty-seven, succumbed to cardiac arrest in Calcutta, the Indian city where she had created the Order of Missionaries of Charity.

Their completely different worlds notwithstanding, these two great-hearted women showed the world how to give meaning to life by caring for others. "It is the great lesson that they leave us," declared President Bill Clinton in his homage "to these two exceptional women."

Entirely opposite, and yet Diana and Mother Teresa were bound by the same concern: the recognition of dignity and value in every human being, including those who are too often forgotten, those in misery, who have been abandoned, the sick, the dying.

When she left Mother Teresa after her most recent visit to New York in June 1997, Diana radiated happiness and love. Bending over the tiny nun, who only came up to her chest, she had felt all the force that emanated from this being, who was for Diana a model of charity.

Opposite:
New York, June 1997.

"Goodbye, England's Rose"

Diana's funeral was held in London on Saturday, September 6, 1997; it was a deeply moving service, held in Westminster Abbey. Millions of Britons followed the tribute, lining the funeral route and assembling in Hyde Park to watch the proceedings on giant television screens. Millions more watched at home, a billion worldwide.

The two thousand guests gathered in the Abbey perfectly illustrated the personality of this princess, united in friendship with many artists. Singers Elton John, Sting, and George Michael, actors Tom Cruise and his wife, Nicole Kidman, and tenor Luciano Pavarotti were in attendance.

No crowned heads. Hillary Clinton represented the United States and Bernadette Chirac, France. Also present were heads of various charities that Diana was committed to.

The hour-long service began with the national anthem, "God Save the Queen." At the piano, tears in his eyes, Elton John sang "Goodbye, England's Rose," adapted from the song "Candle in the Wind," which he wrote with Bernie Taupin as a posthumous tribute to Marilyn Monroe and whose lyrics he transformed into an homage to Diana.

Among the other guests were the country's chief political representatives, above all Prime Minister Tony Blair, who read from I Corinthians, the New Testament text on fraternal love. Diana had "profoundly influenced this nation and the world," declared the Dean of Westminster, Wesley Carr, as he opened the ceremony.

And indeed, all along the funeral route, one could, in effect, gauge just how much Diana, with her charisma and her caring, had touched the whole country and beyond.

The coffin was drawn on a gun carriage pulled by six horses, accompanied by soldiers of the Welsh Guard. It was brought to Westminster Abbey after a long tour, followed on foot part of the way by Princes William, fifteen, and Harry, twelve (just ten days before his thirteenth birthday), as well as by Prince Charles; their grandfather, the Duke of Edinburgh; and Earl Spencer, Diana's brother. For about half an hour the two young princes, their faces set, walked silently behind their mother's coffin to the tolling of a bell. They tried to hide their pain by lowering their heads, but tears were streaming down their cheeks. The immense, silent crowd sustained them throughout the procession, throwing flowers as the cortege passed.

For the first time in the history of the kingdom, the Union Jack was flown at half-staff above Buckingham Palace, thus preempting the royal family's traditional standard. The massive crowd of subjects long applauded the national flag.

On the coffin, draped with the royal standard, were a bouquet of white lilies from Earl Spencer, a wreath of white tulips from Prince William, and one of white roses from Prince Harry accompanied by a card addressed to "Mummy."

That afternoon Princess Diana was buried in strictest privacy on the Spencer estate, Althorp, about seventy miles north of London. Except for Charles and his sons, the royal family was not in attendance.

Diana lies on a little grassy isle in the middle of an artificial lake, far from all the curiosity seekers.

Pages 160–164: Diana's funeral, September 6, 1997.

164